ISBN 978-1-5281-6266-1
PIBN 10930899

For support please visit www.forgottenbooks.com

English
Français
Deutsche
Italiano
Español
Português

www.forgottenbooks.com

Mythology Photography **Fiction**
Fishing Christianity **Art** Cooking
Essays Buddhism Freemasonry
Medicine **Biology** Music **Ancient
Egypt** Evolution Carpentry Physics
Dance Geology **Mathematics** Fitness
Shakespeare **Folklore** Yoga Marketing
Confidence Immortality Biographies
Poetry **Psychology** Witchcraft
Electronics Chemistry History **Law**
Accounting **Philosophy** Anthropology
Alchemy Drama Quantum Mechanics
Atheism Sexual Health **Ancient History**
Entrepreneurship Languages Sport
Paleontology Needlework Islam
Metaphysics Investment Archaeology
Parenting Statistics Criminology
Motivational

ANNUAL ADDRESS

DELIVERED BEFORE THE

MEDICAL SOCIETY OF THE STATE OF CALIFORNI

— BY —

GERRARD GEORGE TYRRELL,

Member of the King and Queen's College of Physicians, Ireland; Licentiate of
the Royal College of Surgeons, Ireland; Member of the American
Medical Association, President of the Society.

SACRAMENTO, CAL.

SACRAMENTO :
Day & Joy, Printers, 1023 Eighth Street.
1882.

THE ANNUAL ADDRESS.

By GERRARD GEORGE TYRRELL, M. K. & Q. C. P., I., L. R. C. S., I., L. M.

PRESIDENT OF THE SOCIETY.

LADIES AND GENTLEMEN OF THE MEDICAL SOCIETY OF THE
STATE OF CALIFORNIA: The most pleasing part of my duty in
addressing you this morning, is to express my grateful thanks
for the honor you have conferred upon me in deeming me
worthy of presiding over this, the largest society of votaries
to science upon the Pacific Coast. I assure you that I appre-
ciate the extent of your partiality to the utmost, and trust
that in carrying out your wishes as your presiding officer, I
may so act as to bring with me into my retirement your con-
tinued respect and good will. To hope to address you in an
exhaustive manner upon any particular subject in medicine,
is a task so far beyond my capabilities, or, in truth, my desire,
that I will not essay it, but rather endeavor to secure your
attention while expressing, in an informal manner, a few
thoughts which in the interest of regular medicine have oc-
curred to me within the past year.

It has been remarked that the departed year was one of
unusual interest to the medical profession throughout the
world, chiefly through the impetus given to scientific knowledge by the meeting together in congress of that vast assem-
blage of educated, earnest workers in medicine and skilled
practitioners in surgery, who, coming from all parts of the
civilized world to add to the store of knowledge already in
our possession, have afforded us an example of the unselfishness
of our profession, and how ready it is to sacrifice personal
interest in the cause of humanity. In a smaller way as to
members, but upon an equality in principle, may we regard

70165

the annual gathering of our Society. Here we have students
of nature and votaries to science from all parts of this great
State, leaving their mountain homes, where their services are
always requisite and always valuable, or taking long and toil-
some journeys over the lowland plains or sandy wastes, generally sacrificing their pecuniary interests, that they may here
spread the truth they know, or learn from others the truths
they have to tell. All are met for one purpose—to demon-
strate the power of truth, to strengthen each other in the pur-
suit of knowledge, and the universal desire to advance the
cause of civilization by making known what they have learned
in the great laboratory of nature towards saving life, allevi-
ating suffering, or, greatest of all, preventing disease.

"Medicine," said the late philosopher and accomplished
physician, Maurice Reynaud, "is a matter not of faith, but of
knowledge, and its precepts have no other value than that
which our reason accords to them." It is this fact that
makes our science and our art progressive. We must have
knowledge, and such knowledge that the reasoning power
with which we are endowed does not revolt against it. It
must have truth for its basis, and honesty in its belief. To
scientific medicine, elaborated out of the accumulated wisdom
of ages, do we owe all that is known, not only of the causation
of disease, but also of its mode of cure. This "science of im-
provement" still continues from inductive premises to deduc-
tive fact, benefiting the art of medicine, and, by the bright
light of science and of truth, revealing the wonders of ani-
mated nature, scattering the gloom of superstitions and beliefs
in the mystery of disease, and proving that beneath its phe-
nomena we have agencies at work operating in accordance
with natural law, and that through such law alone can we hope
to arrest or prevent it. When we reflect upon the researches
of Pasteur, Drysdale, Klebs, Koch, Klein, Sanderson, Cru-
velli, and a host of others in the field of experimental physi-
ology, pregnant as they are with the grandest results, we seem
to be approaching the very verge of a discovery which will
so vastly increase our sway over those diseases in whose pres-

ence we now stand almost powerless, that in time we may practically arrest and exterminate them. In view of this fact, how childish and silly does it seem to us, armed with a knowledge of the past, and apparently an ever widening field of newly discovered truths before us in the future, to hear intelligent people remark that we regularly educated physicians belong to the "old school," as though our art were a thing of the dead past, and not pulsating with the onward surging wave of the living present; to tell *us* that all that is new and progressive in medicine came into existence through the infinitesimal nothingness of what this generation in its wisdom is pleased to call the "new school," whose disciples are making such earnest and persistent efforts toward recognition by regular practitioners, encouraged in their endeavor since Dr. Bristow, in his now famous address before the British Medical Association, at Ryde, promulgated the idea that association in consultation with homeopaths is possible without loss of dignity or self-respect. Happily for science, this strange and derogatory doctrine was instantly and decisively repudiated by the profession of Great Britain, and the address condemned, as not representative of its ideas, by the association in which it took its rise. I would not have alluded to this subject had not an address been sent to me as one delivered before a California Medical Society, in which, while admiring and acknowledging its literary ability, and earnestly indorsing many of the salient points contained therein, I find sufficient evidence to assure me that this leveling down doctrine had reached the Pacific Coast, as the following extract will show. The author having quoted and cordially subscribed to that portion of Dr. Bristow's address in which he makes a special plea for breaking down the barriers which now separate regular from irregular medicine, and which Hahnemann declared to be an "impassable gulf," says:

"I am not sure that the representatives of the homeopathic faith in this city are behind the regular practitioner in intelligence, education, and gentlemanly bearing; and however much my reason may rebel against their peculiar postulates, it cannot be denied that they possess the confidence of no inconsiderable portion of the community. To be forever posing in a militant attitude toward them is not conducive to the elevation of medical morals. The proposal to consult with them at the bedside has raised no little outcry in orthodox circles, but it is difficult to see where the valid objection lies. The regular physician who consents to see a patient in company with his homeopathic attendant need be in no fear but that, while working together, the doctrine of Hahnemann will be left entirely out of sight. Indeed, the educated homeopathist is rather inclined to laugh at these doctrines, so far from taking them as his guide. It is surprising how well acquainted he will prove to be with the principles of legitimate medicine, and how little real antagonism he entertains toward them. To consult with one of our own faith who still clings to methods and beliefs long superseded, is often a far more difficult matter."

It will perhaps be a matter of surprise to learn that this quotation is from the pen of a professor in one of our honored Universities, and the President of one of the San Francisco Medical Societies. Emanating from such a source, it demands our most respectful consideration, containing, as it does, the expression of a tendency toward the renunciation of those principles upon which legitimate medicine has taken its stand, and which have carried it to the exalted position it now occupies in the history of the world, viz: truth, honor, honesty, justice, experience, observation, and scientific fact. To present this matter fairly, we will analyze the quotation into the several reasons given by the distinguished author against which no valid objection can lie to debar us from meeting homeopathic practitioners at the bedside.

First—They are not behind the regular practitioner in education, intelligence, or gentlemanly bearing.

Second—Although reason rebels against their peculiar postulates, they enjoy the confidence of no inconsiderable portion of the community.

Third—A militant attitude toward them is not conducive to medical morality.

Fourth—That in consultation, Hahnemann and his doctrines will be ignored, and in addition, will be laughed at by the homeopathic attendant.

Fifth — Because you will be surprised how much your homeopathist knows of the principles of regular medicine, and how much humbug there is in his antagonism to them.

Sixth—It is easier to consult with an educated homeopath than a physician in regular standing whose beliefs are antiquated, and whose methods are superseded.

Let us follow these reasons to their legitimate conclusion. To the first reason given there can be no valid objection, if the assumption were only true, which our experience leads us to deny; but to say that we can consult with a man against whose postulates our reason rebels, and whose pretensions we know to be a falsehood, because he has the confidence of no inconsiderable portion of the community, is asking us to countenance a fraud, in order that we may pocket a fee. If this is to be our rule of conduct, why not consult with Lipotai, or similar Chinese impostors, with magnetic healers or spiritual doctors, or electro-plated therapeutists, and other charlatans, who also share a large portion of the confidence of the public not only here, but in every other city upon the Pacific Coast? If consultation is to be made upon the basis that the homeopath, being an intelligent, educated gentleman, will, at the bedside, ignore Hahnemann, laugh at his doctrines, surprise us with his appreciation of the principles of regular medicine, and to oppose his pretensions is rebellion against medical morality, then are we to make ourselves participators in the criminal deceit of consulting with a man who is pretending to be what he is not—professing homeopathy to his confiding patient, and laughing at its absurdities to his presumably honest consultant. Truly, this is a morality that cannot be very elevating to the medical standard of our profession, as seen by disinterested parties. The last plea for fraternization is, if possible, less defensible than any—that it is easier to consult with an educated homeopath who has no faith in his own practice, and pretends to have no faith in ours, than to advise with a regularly educated physician who still clings to methods and beliefs long since superseded, which would of necessity include those who still believe that bleeding is often beneficial in disease, and that a dose of calomel has some depurative action upon the liver. From this analysis I think it will be conceded by every fair thinking man that all the arguments used by the author of the San Francisco address for fraternization with homeopathists, are in truth the most convincing reasons why we should *not* meet these gentlemen in consultation. We cannot, in honor and honesty, meet them if they are homeopathists, because there can be no interchange of ideas where hopeless incompatibility of principles exist—their notions of pathology and therapeutics being fundamentally contradictory and antagonistic to ours.

"If, for the purpose of securing patronage, the homeopathist pretends to a superior system in which he does not believe, and to a better practice which he does not follow, he is a charlatan and a pretender, unworthy of confidence or honorable association. If a regular physician, for the sake of a consultation fee, or for the purpose of obtaining popular favor, sacrifices his convictions, relinquishes measures in which he has confidence, and consents to a practice he is sure is useless, he may be a fitting person for such consultations, but he is not an honorable member of an honorable profession. If between an honest homeopath and an equally honest regular physician there can be no agreement and co-operation in the treatment of a case, consultations between such are certainly useless. No opinion need be expressed respecting consultations between parties one or both of whom are insincere. Should the homeopathist abandon his system, or the regular physician embrace it, there may be harmony and agreement, but until then, consistency and honor, no less than proper professional feeling, will forbid the unnatural alliance."—*Professor A. B. Palmer, North American Review.*

I find that at the last meeting of the Medical Society of the State of New York, this very question of consultation with homeopaths formed part of the presidential address. In his opinion there was an objection to meeting any man who. was not satisfied with the simple name of physician or medical man. He further says: "This question of consultation has often been raised. It was claimed that the sick man had a right to select his doctor. Certainly, but the doctor has also a right to select his patient. The patient knew beforehand that he could not expect a consultation between his homeopathic attendant and one of us, and he took his choice. From his youngest days onward he had but one rule, and that was to be governed by the law of his profession—so long as these laws exist, obey them. If the majority does not wish to obey them any longer, abolish them when the time has come. It is asserted by many that this time has come, and that there are good reasons for abolishing the boundaries between the several *classes* of medical men. I do not speak of *schools* of medical men, for modern medicine is not divided into schools. If we have reason to believe not only that medical science is one and indivisible, and based upon logic and experimentation, but that the profession of the State of New York are sufficiently imbued with that spirit of logic and experimental science, we may overlook differences, and meet with a spirit of reconciliation those who do not encounter us any more with the dicta of a school or sect."

This expression of opinion is, I think, in consonance with the ideas of every thinking medical man. We do not pose in a militant attitude against those homeopaths who are homeopaths, honest in their belief—we ignore them; but we do oppose those who, calling themselves homeopaths, are using the name, not as an exposition of their practice, but for the purpose of trade—a means of obtaining the confidence and patronage of the public, which, under the simple name of physician, would be denied to all whose educational acquirements were not of an order that would demand recognition at the hands of an intelligent community. I have been somewhat

2

elaborate upon this vexed question, because I believe that in the presence upon this coast of such a seeming dallying with this quintessence of imposture, as appears in the address I have made the subject of these remarks, that it was my duty to mention it before this Society. The question will come before the National Medical Association at its next meeting, and we should be prepared to define our position upon it. We must either emulate the noble example of Germany, who, by its Central Committee resolved "that it is self-evident that medical men cannot consult with those who call themselves homeopaths," or, with Great Britain, determine to have nothing to do with anything in medicine that savors of fraud, deception, or trifling with truth, or we must abide the inevitable disastrous result.

The science of medicine is knowledge, not faith; and whenever, for expediency, popularity, or pecuniary reward, we travel outside the domain of knowledge or theory that we believe to be true, then do we rightly and justly forfeit the esteem and confidence of the public who has trusted and confided in our honor and honesty, and sink beneath the level of the most unprincipled quack whose only motive and highest ambition is that of being a successful knave. "Nothing," says the able editor of the *London Lancet*, "is so much needed, just now, as the rise in our midst of a stern and uncompromising apostle of sincerity in science—a man of unpitying animosity to humbug in all its forms, who will not hesitate at any bidding to denounce wrong doing and untruthfulness, let who may be the offender. It is time that a spirit of manliness went out in our ranks to chase away the lying spirit of mock courtesy—this faint-hearted and time-serving sentimentality which makes us so ready to look kindly upon any pretender, and so reluctant to expose any pretense." I cordially coincide with the sentiment expressed in these brave words by this brave editor. The time has come when we must cease dallying with this wanton spirit of mock courtesy and time-serving sentimentality that would make us forget the glorious history of our art, with all its attendant triumphs, to do honor to a fiction in science, an imposition on credulity, and accept upon equality the *traders* in a name. I believe that I have now explicitly defined my position upon this subject without fear, favor, or mental reservation. I am utterly opposed to professional consultation with any man who assumes a distinctive title to adopt any exclusive system of medicine, as rational medicine knows none. I am opposed to quackery in any form, regular or irregular; have always opposed it, and will continue to do so whenever and wherever I can. The science of medicine needs nó pretense to establish its truth, no mystery to enhance its merit, no falsehood to make known its claims. It stands to-day the immortal testament of our progress, the holiest temple of our civilization.

Trusting that the views here enunciated will meet with the approval of the Medical Society of the State of California, a Society so remarkable since its inception for the steadfast, earnest manner in which it has sought to elevate to the highest standard the professional dignity and honor of its members, I would respectfully suggest and recommend that our delegates to the American Medical Association be instructed, if the question should arise and be discussed, to protest earnestly and emphatically against any change in the American Code of Medical Ethics, in so far as it relates to the matter of consultation with irregular practitioners.

I now desire to bring under your notice as briefly as possible a subject which may perhaps be trenching somewhat upon the prerogative of the State Board of Health, but which nevertheless is of such importance to the welfare of the community that I may be pardoned in desiring to hear an expression of opinion from this Society upon it. I refer to the frequency of zymotic diseases as a result of poisoning by sewer gas, which obtains circulation in our buildings and dwellings through the agency of imperfect or defective plumbing, and the necessity that exists of obtaining such legislation as will eventuate in placing the entire control of the plumbing and drainage of our buildings and dwellings, as far as their efficiency and safety is concerned, in the hands of the Boards of Health. Such a law at present exists in the City of New York, by which the plumbing and drainage of all buildings, both public and private, is executed in accordance with plans previously approved, in writing, by the Board of Health, who are also authorized to receive and place on file drawings and descriptions of the plumbing and drainage of buildings, erected previous to the passage of the Act, in their respective cities. A law somewhat similar has been enacted in the District of Columbia, also in Pennsylvania, and I believe in Maryland. In the District of Columbia the Commissioners, on recommendation of the Health Officer, appoint an Inspector of Plumbing, to inspect all houses in course of erection, and pass upon their plumbing and sewerage. A refusal to comply with the requirements of the Act is punishable by a fine of from $25 to $200, or imprisonment for thirty days. The law proposed for Pennsylvania provided that after the passage of the Act no dwelling or building was to be occupied, for any purpose whatsoever, until the Inspector had decided, after due examination, that its drainage and plumbing were perfectly secure, and furnished a certificate attesting the same. When we reflect upon the number of valuable lives that are yearly sacrificed by the directly poisonous effluvia emanating from defective or obstructed sewage, broken pipes, inefficient joints, useless traps, and other evils attendant upon dishonest plumbing, the subject gains additional interest, and seems well worthy the serious attention of this Society.

Dr. Baylis, in his work upon house drainage, says: "If we look for the cause of the large mortality from zymotic diseases in our cities, we find it principally in sewer gas poisoning. Other causes operate to swell the total, but to bad plumbing work we may attribute the prevalence of pythogenic pneumonia, peritonitis, inflammatory rheumatism, typhoid fever, croup, diphtheria, and many kindred diseases which are almost epidemic in all our large cities. Unfortunately for the progress of sanitary reform, the difference between good and bad plumbing work is usually so slight as to escape the notice of any but a trained expert, but it is commonly great enough to exert an active and far-reaching power for mischief.'' Having, then, described the pipe system of an average New York house of the better sort, he comes to the conclusion that everything was so favorable to sewer gas poisoning that he no longer wondered at the great mortality from disease of pythogenic origin, and thinks that as the plumbing work is commonly done, it would be better for most of us if we had to bring our water in buckets from a public hydrant, and carry our waste to the culvert at the nearest street corner. As he truly says, the plumber's work is covered by the builder, and at once hidden from sight. In a few weeks or months the occupant of the house complains of an obstructed sewer, a leak in the soil pipe, a troublesome odor that cannot be accounted for, or some other of the numerous evils that follow in the wake of "scamped" plumbing. The Inspector investigates, and finds a pipe of insufficient size, the joints put together with common mortar, instead of cement, improperly laid, so that the joints have opened; a pipe perhaps broken in the laying left with an opening for the escape of gases; no trap, perhaps, under sink or closet, or the bathtub connection with soil pipe below the trap. These defects he finds of everyday occurrence. Such facts as these, and from such authority, should impress us with the magnitude of the evil we have to suppress, as we cannot expect that any of our large cities enjoy any greater immunity from dishonest work, or, charitably speaking, from ignorance of the principles of sanitary security, than New York or Philadelphia, or other well ordered city; and when we learn from Dr. Maypother, of Dublin, that of the one hundred and forty thousand cases of typhoid fever which occur annually in England, of which twenty thousand terminate fatally, which are clearly traceable to defective drainage and sewer gas poisoning—and yet that is but one of a long list of prevailing zymotic diseases—we can see how highly important it is that we, as conservators of public health, should exert our whole influence toward the mitigation, if we cannot to the suppression, of this preventable destruction of human life. In fact, we might indorse the opinion of the

Health Officer of the District of Columbia, who, in speaking of this provision for sanitary inspection, says: "That such a law does not stand prominent upon the pages of the code of every city, is a disgraceful reproach upon the intelligence and civilization of the present age." I would therefore suggest, that as it is expedient that every city or town provided with a system of sewerage should have provision made for the proper inspection, by an expert officer appointed by the State Board of Health, of the plumbing and drainage of all houses and buildings connected with its sewerage, that the Committee on Medical Legislation be requested to take this matter under their consideration, with a view of procuring such legislative action as they may deem necessary to attain the desired result.

Another subject presents itself to my mind to which I am desirous of calling your attention for a few moments, as it is one that is universally forcing itself upon the consideration of the thinking portion of the community, and which I believe may appropriately be taken cognizance of by this Society. I allude to the necessity which exists for the proper provision by the State, of some suitable establishment for the safe custody of insane criminals, and those who, under the plea of insanity, are acquitted of atrocious crime. The increase that has taken place in this class of criminals, not only in this, but in other States of the Union, is apparent to the most casual observer. Whether this is the result of our greater familiarity with the different phases of a diseased brain, and our ability to detect them in their obscurer forms, or from the frequency with which this mental defect is brought before the public, and hence are rendered more familiar with it, or from the facility with which such persons escape from the restraining hand of justice and are allowed to return to liberty after the solemn declaration of their insanity by a jury of their countrymen, it is evident that the means at present provided for their proper care and treatment are inadequate and unsatisfactory. In an address delivered before this Society nearly ten years ago, by that distinguished alienist, and your presiding officer, Dr. G. A. Shurtleff, he clearly discerned then that the whole question of the trial, custody, and treatment of the criminal insane needed revision. At that time the State was startled, as it has been since, by the committal of atrocious crime which escaped its just punishment upon the plea of insanity. The law was inadequate or defective, which elicited from Dr. Shurtleff the following pertinent remarks. He says:

"There should be a change in our laws respecting the criminal insane. Upon the acquittal of a person charged with murder, on the ground of insanity, the killing being admitted or proven, it should be the duty of the Judge trying the case to commit such insane homicide, regardless of his mental condition at the time of trial, to an asylum for the insane, where he should be securely kept. And there should be no authority vested in any officer of the asylum to discharge patients of this class by reason of their apparent recovery or sanity. Such a provision of law would render the plea of insanity less frequent and the community more secure."

Again:

"The frequency with which the plea of insanity has of late been resorted to, with undeserved success, to avoid responsibility for crime—the irregular, unscientific, and generally unfair manner in which such trials are conducted with regard to medical testimony—the danger of a more unenlightened, misguided, reactionary movement, to the peril of the really insane—the ends of justice and the welfare of society, all seem to call for reform in the law relating to the trial of criminal cases in which the mental condition of the accused is involved."

Under the Penal Code of California, as it stands to-day, the disposition of these cases is as follows. Under Section 1167 it says: "If the jury render a verdict of acquittal on the ground of insanity, the Court may order a jury to be summoned to inquire whether the defendant continues to be insane; and the Court may order him detained in custody until the question of his insanity is determined. If this jury find the defendant is then insane, he shall be committed by the

Sheriff to the State Insane Asylum; but if the jury find the defendant sane, he shall be discharged."

Under Section 1368: "When the case is called, or during the trial, or when defendant is brought up for judgment, or if a doubt arises as to the sanity of the defendant, the Court may order a jury to try the question."

The next section prescribes how he shall be tried. Section 1370 says: "If the jury find the defendant sane, the trial must proceed; if insane, the trial or judgment must be suspended until he become sane, and in the meantime he is committed to the State Insane Asylum, where he is retained until he become sane."

According to the Penal Code, then, a man charged with murder, and being acquitted upon the ground of insanity, is discharged, except he give evidence after his acquittal that he is still insane, when he is again tried upon that question solely, and if the jury do not consider that he is then insane, he is discharged. The result of this law is the attempt of nearly every criminal, charged with murder or other atrocious crime, to escape punishment, upon the plea of temporary or emotional insanity. If he can only succeed in making a jury believe that he was insane at the time of the committal of the crime, his freedom is assured, as the law says he must be discharged. Another jury, if summoned, has only to try the question whether he is then insane, and if it says he is not, he must be discharged. Can we wonder, then, at the number of dreadful murderers who have escaped justice under such a law? The question arises before us to-day, as it did eighty years ago before Lord Kenyon, in the trial of Hatfield—"how are we to dispose of the prisoner? For his own sake," said Lord Kenyon, "and for the sake of society at large, he must not be discharged, for this is a case that concerns every man of every station, from the King upon the throne to the beggar at the gate. People of both sexes and all ages may, in an unfortunate hour, fall a sacrifice to this man who is not under the guidance of sound reason; and, therefore, it is absolutely necessary, for the safety of society, that he shall be properly vision for the strict confinement of such persons, during his Majesty's pleasure, under what is known as "The Insane Offenders Bill." This bill was rendered necessary, from the fact that the statute law was so defective that it had been found that persons who had committed the most shocking acts, and been acquitted on the ground of being deranged in their intellect, had been again allowed to go at large, and again committed similar atrocities. Under this statute the law was administered until after the trial of Oxford, for shooting at the Queen, when it was found that his case did not come under the meaning of the statute, which necessitated the passing of another Act (3 and 4 Vic., Chap. 54), entitled "An Act for making further provision for the confinement and maintenance of insane prisoners." Under its provisions the Secretary of State is empowered, under certain formalities, to grant a warrant by which any insane person can be removed into safe custody, and under the same Act is authorized, under like restrictions, to grant the release from confinement, or the discharge of such person. Under this warrant a criminal lunatic may, under certain conditions, regain his liberty; but when the royal warrant is issued, it virtually means detention during life. This warrant is issued in all cases of acquittal for murder on the plea of insanity, and in all the higher class of crimes—treason, etc.

It is an axiom in law, admitted by every country, that no man who has committed an offense in an unsound state of mind, shall be held responsible for his conduct. "But," says Mr. Hurlbut, one of the Supreme Judges of the State of New York, "the law having pronounced an act dangerous to society, the offender must be restrained of his liberty, to prevent its repetition. If the issue be found against the prisoner, the judgment of the tribunal should be, that he be lodged in a

3

safe place of confinement provided by the State for prisoners of this person's description, there to remain under appropriate treatment for his moral and intellectual condition until he be discharged under due course of law." "If the plea of insanity," continues Mr. Hurlbut, "be made out the prisoner is found not guilty, and discharged out of custody. His act may have been a homicide, occasioned by the destructive mania. The disposition to kill may be still as strong as ever, and the jury know it, and the Court trembles when it discharges him, lest he should kill others. This verdict does not imply that he has not slain a fellow being; does not mean that he is a safe man to go at large; on the contrary, by reason of his mania, he is the most dangerous of men. But what the jury mean by a verdict of acquittal is, that he is not a proper subject for punishment." Under such practical observations as these and others, which time will not permit me to quote, the Asylum for Insane Convicts was established at Auburn, New York— the first, and I believe the only separate establishment of the kind in the country. Its admirable workings, and the excellent policy which founded it, are recognized and acknowledged wherever the question of provision for insane criminals has received attention.

In California the prisoner is discharged, or sent, if insane, to one of the State Insane Asylums, where escape is easy, as these institutions are charitable, and not penal, and cannot be so guarded as to render escape impossible. It is well known that an insane criminal, who retains his cunning, is, under the most favorable circumstances, a much more difficult person to guard than one who is sane, and consequently his chances of getting away are increased in proportion; but to the criminal who feigns insanity, the insane asylum offers itself as the safest, easiest, and most certain road to freedom that can present itself. But, waiving all these considerations, the question may be asked: Is it right to send an insane convict, or a person acquitted of murder on the plea of insanity, to our State Insane Asylums? The law says: "When a prisoner is declared insane, he shall be sent there.'' Dr. Shurtleff, in his report to the Directors of the State Insane Asylum, for 1873, says:

"There have been, within the period of my superintendency, in all forty-six patients transferred from San Quentin to Stockton. Among them were murderers, highway robbers, burglars, thieves, and the perpetrators of other atrocious crimes. Some of them, in their physical outlines, no less than by their vicious lives, illustrate a brutalized degeneracy reached only through a long course of ancestral debasement. They are generally familiar with all the low slang, mischievous acts, and common vices usually prevalent in the haunts of criminals. Mental disease does not deprive them of these bad attainments, nor wholly destroy their natural characteristics. It seldom changes them for the better, or renders their influence other than pernicious. The murderer, becoming insane, is more disposed to homicidal violence than is the good law-abiding citizen with the same mental affection. So the insane thief is more likely to steal than the patient who, before his insanity, had respected the rights and property of others; and the burglar, unless stupid from dementia, or a purposeless maniac, is almost certain to contrive the means of picking locks, and of making his escape from the asylum. He is also very likely to teach others his troublesome art. In spite of the closest confinement and the best security consistent with asylum discipline, twenty-five per cent of our convict patients have escaped. The influence of this class of patients upon others is incalculably bad in every respect. But,'' continues Dr. Shurtleff, "by this incompatible mixture a still greater wrong is done to the other inmates socially. By compulsion, and without fault of their own, they are made the associates of convicted felons. We must not suppose the insane are stolid and indifferent as to their moral and social position; on the contrary, they are frequently rendered more acutely sensitive to every apparent disrespect or derogation. Indeed, I question the moral right, though the Legislature has arbitrarily established the legal one, to force upon the society of the honorable and upright, who are secluded from the public by the misfor-

tune of sickness, the convicted felon who has been excluded
from the general society of his fellow-beings solely on account
of his crimes.   To do so is to tantalize misfortune and add a
needless shame to affliction."

Dr. Dewey, Physician to the Illinois State Insane Asylum,
speaking of the unfitness of insane criminals for association
with the insane who are free from crime, after enumerating
the crimes of those placed under his charge, says:

"Is not the moral infection of such as these in. the asylum
as much to be dreaded as any physical infection?   If one
sickly sheep can infect the flock, how much pestilence will
these moral lepers bring with them?   Are not the misfortunes
of the insane already sufficient, without subjecting them to
this further degradation?   Is it possible to suppose that the
people of any community or State into whose families the
ominous specter of insanity sooner or later stalks, wish the
afflicted ones to dwell familiarly with such companions?   Insanity but seldom renders its victims better than before, in any
respect; more generally, indeed, it adds darker and more re-
pulsive features to the character.   They are more prone than
the rest of the insane to commit dangerous and violent acts;
to be concocting plans of escape, rebellion, or mutiny; to tor-
ment the feeble and irascible about them; to teach new les-
sons in depravity to the pupils so easily found around them."

From these extracts, which might be multiplied, from the
experiences of every physician in attendance upon an insane
asylum, we can partially learn how wrong, how unjust, and
how unfit it is to send these criminals, made worse by reason
of their insanity, to our State Insane Asylums.   They cannot
be separated from other insane patients, as our asylums are
not constructed for that purpose, and they cannot be locked
up in their rooms, as that is just what they are sent to the
asylum to escape, because it is unjust and inhuman, and would
destroy every hope of recovery.   The asylum has no machinery,
and should need none, such as is required for the safe keeping
of this class.

That our State Prison, as at present constituted, is not a proper place for the custody or confinement of these unfortunates, is conclusively shown in the report of Dr. Pelham, formerly Physician to the Prison at San Quentin; in his report for 1877 he says: "The prison is destitute of proper accommodation for the insane. * * * At present they are confined in cells in the main cell building, and are not separated from the other prisoners except by cell walls, and they often render night hideous by their ravings, thus disturbing the sleep of others, and those who must labor during the day. To avoid this state of affairs, there is at present but one remedy—the dungeon—which has frequently to be used for this purpose. With the present accommodations for the treatment of such cases, results are unsatisfactory and remedial measures cannot be resorted to with reasonable prospect of success."

From this extract we may learn that no proper place exists in our prison for the care or treatment of these insane criminals. It is not right or just to keep a noisy maniac within the wards of an hospital among cases of sickness where absolute quiet is required; neither ought the nineteenth century civilization permit the thrusting of a raving maniac within the walls of a dark and noisome dungeon, deprived of light and wholesome air, perhaps chained to its damp and reeking floor, to preserve from harm its other and more sane inmates. The only remedy presented to us to obviate this manifest and glaring wrong to our fellow-beings, who, although insane, are not criminal, and to those who are both criminal and insane, is a separate and special provision for the care and custody of the criminal insane, and this in the erection by the State of a suitable asylum, constituted and adapted to this special purpose, since the inmates intended for its occupancy, although insane, are still dangerous outlaws and criminals, retaining for the most part all their criminal characteristics and vicious proclivities. More especially is this required from the want of adequate room for the proper care of the ordinarily insane, our asylums now being filled far beyond their sanitary capacity. It is the opinion of those who are interested in the welfare of the insane, and have written upon the subject, that the preferable location for such an asylum would be within the precincts of our State prisons, and not in connection with hospitals or asylums for the ordinarily insane. At Folsom, within our prison grounds, is an admirable location for such an asylum; there is plenty of room, a genial climate, a generous soil that would afford plenty of occupation in cultivating and adorning it. Its construction might be accomplished at a minimum cost by utilizing prison labor; the material is right on the ground, and its medical management might safely be intrusted to the medical officer of the prison. Within its walls should be confined, for life, all those dangerous homicides who are acquitted upon the plea of insanity, and also all those who offer the same defense for other equally atrocious crimes. All those who become insane after their arrest and before their trial, should also be committed to this asylum, as well as those who become mentally deranged after trial and conviction, or who are serving out their term of punishment. This would at once relieve our State insane asylums of this very undesirable class of patients, and of their over-crowded condition, and release our prisons from the necessity of keeping insane convicts locked in their cells or thrust into dungeons, to the disgrace of our civilization.

The Penal Code should be so amended that upon the trial of any person for murder or other capital offense, and his insanity at the time of committing the offense is given in evidence, as a plea against punishment, and the jury acquit him, the jury ought to be required to find *specially* whether he was insane at the time of the commission of the offense, and declare whether he was acquitted on account of such insanity; and if the jury find that he was, and was acquitted on those grounds, then the Court should have no other alternative than that of committing the defendant to the asylum for the criminal insane for the term of his natural life, regardless of his mental condition at the time of rendering the verdict. For the sufficient reason, that no guarantee can be offered or accepted, by the prisoner or his friends, that a recurrence of his emotional, impulsive, inspirational, moral, or temporary, or any other insanity upon which he may have been acquitted, will not take place at any moment thereafter, to the danger of the community or the life of an individual. If the plea were true, the prisoner is certainly one of the most dangerous of men to be at large; and if false, and only used by the defense with legal ingenuity, as a means of swaying the minds of a susceptible jury, the punishment of incarceration for life would be no greater than such a criminal would deserve. Such a change in the organic law would at once put a stop to those travesties of justice we have so often, and so lately, witnessed in our Courts of law, and prevent the plea of insanity from being used to defend, or cover up, some of the most revolting and atrocious crimes that have ever disgraced the annals of the State.

The provisions of those sections of our Civil Code respecting the examination of persons alleged to be insane before juries, and assisted by counsel, should be amended or repealed, and also the mode of medical examination by hypothetical questions, it being impossible for the medical witness to fairly present his opinion to the Court and jury by this mode of putting questions. The principle by which medical experts are compelled to attend Courts of law without adequate compensation is unjust and unfair; the physician's special knowledge being his private property, which, if taken from him by the State, ought to be paid for. This subject demands investigation and a legal remedy by the Legislature.

Superior Judges should be empowered to allow such extra compensation to medical experts summoned in criminal cases as in their judgment would be adequate and just; to fix the amount, and order it paid out of the funds of the County Treasury. Judges only should have the power of appointing medical experts; or better still, medical experts should be officers of the Government, as are the Judges whom they assist. Their appointment should be permanent to secure impartiality, they should be rigidly examined to secure their competency, and they should be well paid to secure the ability necessary to the office. Thus only will experts be had whose views are not pre-ascertained in favor of prosecution or defense, and we spared the humiliation of seeing brought into Court two sets of witnesses, each impliedly under contract to render his best services in the interest of the party by whom he is paid, or through the influence of personal friends or professional bias. There are some other reforms in the medico-legal jurisprudence of this State which might be inaugurated with great propriety and justice, and in strict consonance with the civilization of the present century; time will not, however, permit me to bring them before you upon this occasion. I would therefore respectfully recommend that the Committee on Medical Legislation be requested to take this whole subject matter under its consideration, with a view of obtaining such legislative action as will result in the establishment of a suitable asylum in this State for the medical care and proper custody of its criminal insane; also, procure such amendments to our Penal Code, that an acquittal for murder by a jury on the plea of insanity, temporary or otherwise, will not mean a discharge from custody and a return to freedom, but will insure the proper security and care of the maniac, and the safety of the community, together with such other alterations, amendments, and revisions of our Codes, both Civil and Penal, that will hereafter place the profession of medicine in a position worthy of its high calling in Courts of law.

During the past year I regret to say that the dread destroyer death has not passed us by. We have to mourn the loss of the young and zealous Matson, who, in the morning of life, was removed from among us. We will also miss the kindly smile and genial welcome of our old and honored member, Wm. Bamford, whose interest in the welfare of this Society never wavered, and whose words of wisdom we cannot forget. Let us cherish their memory, and while we throw the mantle of charity over their faults, if any they had, let us try and emulate the many good, noble, and manly qualities which were common to both.

I cannot close this address without congratulating the Society upon the success which has marked its efforts for the elevation of the medical profession upon this coast. Its proceedings have reflected the highest credit upon its members and placed our young Society far in advance of many of its elder and more pretentious sisters in other States. Let us not be weary in well-doing; continue the good work, and by advancing the cause of scientific medicine, scatter and disperse the misty clouds of ignorance, superstition, and darkness which everywhere surround us, and bring into the full light of day to be seen of all men, the glorious fact, that reason is our guide; that truth, honesty, observation, and experience, combined with knowledge, are the powers by which alone we combat disease, disarm the pallid hand of death, give victory to science, and health to our fellow-men.

SACRAMENTO, April 19, 1882.

9 781528 162668